Ain't I a Woman (Chapbook)
By: Na'Tosha De'Von

Ain't I a Woman
By: Na'Tosha De'Von

Cover Art by:
Jessi Ley

Dedicated to Amy Herzberg, thank you for being the microphone that amplifies small voices in crowded places.

This chap book is an extension of my one woman show called "Ain't I a Woman". Think of these poems as a poetic score that has the capacity to stand alone but are a part of a bigger story. To book and learn more about "Ain't I a Woman" the one person show visit <u>www.natoshadevon.org</u>.

Trigger Warning: This book contains topics on sexual abuse.

Index

10 Things

Ten Things I know about myself to be true
1. I'm a poet
2. I'm a poet who's afraid of my own voice
3. I'm a poet who is afraid of my own voice, so I keep quiet in public places.
4. Keep quiet amongst the spaces. I've kept quiet about the rape.

Ten things I know about myself to be true
1. I'm a poet
2. I'm a poet who's afraid of my own voice
3. I'm a poet who is afraid of my own voice, so I keep quiet in public places. keep quiet amongst the spaces. I've kept quiet about the rape.
4. I repeat myself often because I'm pretty sure no one was listening the

first time. Didn't hear my no's, the STOPS, the refusal to my body.

5. Sometimes I feel more ghost than human, more species than she, more victim than survivor.

6. I once bought a bottle of cologne for my lover. In gratitude, he said "Thank you" In secret it wasn't a gift. The truth is I've never met a lover that doesn't smell like my attacker

7. I only like it rough because I correlate sex with pain. So, pull my hair, put your hands around my throat. Why aren't you slapping me? My first lover slapped me into submission. This is what love should feel like, right?

8. This poem sounds familiar because it reminds you of your sister, your best friend, the freshman girl alone on the bathroom floor you chose not to defend. How uncomfortable this must make you.

9. I don't tell my story often because I'm pretty sure dead horses have already paid their dues

10. This is the part of the poem when I realize that I could have stopped at

nine. You must forgive me. I have a
habit of forcing my presence onto
others the way he forced his body
onto me.

You promise................

I promise

Child's Play

Ok here it goes…… Roses are red Violets are blue Every time you get on the bus, I be watching you. I like the way you smell and the way you blink your eye. When you wore your Dickies outfit, I said dannnggg he so fly. I know we are young and have so much to learn, but when I see you my heart, it burns. I will write your name forever in the sand. Because you will forever be my man.

Disappear

Sometimes I wonder
If I were to ever disappear.
Not disappear, like disappear
but simply disappear
I wonder would you even notice?
Would it bother you?
Would there be a slight shift
in your universe
causing black holes of missing me to
abruptly appear in your galaxy
or would your world stand still?
Would you only notice because the next
person called my name
and there was no answer?
If I left breadcrumb trails of me for you like
Hansel and Gretel
would you step back into your childhood
superhero mentality?
believe that you can fly and risk your cat
nine lives to save me
or would you simply go on with life?
Would there be a change in your everyday
actions
speaking solely upon my actions

that were no longer apparent in your world
You see, I wonder would you even notice?
And if you notice what would you do?
And if you did what would that be
or is it just that ok to live a life filled without
me….
Question, am I disposable?
Or am I simply at your disposal?
Because sometimes I wonder if you need
me or is it I who needs to be needed by you
Can you hold my hand while we play
Jenga and reveal to me the pieces that I
would be in building you up and breaking
you down
Am I your middle piece that you can so
effortlessly remove
or am I your bottom foundation?
And the very thought of removing me
would cause your structure to fall and
break from shaking hands with dying
measures.
Do you even care?
Have you ever?
If you were a tree, would I be your leaf
Could you blow me away with the
seasons or maybe I'm just a branch

and losing me would be just a little bit
harder because that simply means that a part
of you has been broken
but I am hoping that I am your root
And the very impact of stimulation from
me is what ultimately triggers
your growth.
But If I am a root then don't treat me
like a leaf
And if I am a leaf then don't do me any
favors by pretending that I am a branch
because I need to know
what I mean to you.
I need to know my worth
Because sometimes I wonder if I were to
ever disappear
I mean truly disappear
I wonder would you even notice
And if you did
tell me what would you do?

Tangled

During the rape
She won't focus on the stretching
Her insides shape shifting like the
counterparts of Deceptions
She will numb herself from his hands
like noose around her throat
She won't feel, but remember him
Instead, it will be his voice
The broken in his eyes
begging for her approval
Tell me you like it
He will pull out
Stand over her body like the home project
he's been trying to finish
but mommy was too busy to see
So, he grabs the duct tape
Hangs her remains like limp noodle on the
refrigerator for the entire world to see
She's become his masterpiece
He will drag her to the van, go out of his
way to isolate her smile
She then cuts off her ear
Offers it to the Heavens to silence the
sounds of his moans

But God, just like society wants nothing of
her sorrow
It won't be the rejection
But his smell
How his nectar sends out trigger warnings to
fight, flight, or freeze
none in favor of her sanity
so she simply fades away
No need to live in the now when the
memory will metamorph into monsters
The Monsters grow into the night
The night becomes the bed
The bed becomes the sheets
that she once laid on
And now she's forever tangled.

Let his will be Done

Mary never fully gave God permission to
her body
I was told by nameless women in the Bible
that the day he cracked open her purity
for his sacrifice the first rose grew its thorns
After all, when a woman is deflowered in
such a way it makes sense that she'd grow
spikes in order to protect herself
They say her permission was given in a
whisper
Leave it to a man to assume he knows what's
best for you
Glory be to the Father, Son, and Holy spirit
but only grace was given to Mary
What a low blow
The short end of a blessing, the robe of
misogyny
Of course, God is male
Why else are we made to fall upon our
knees in order to please him
There was a reason why the Jezebels in the
Bible were shown God's Mercy
then later filled with his grace
Before this came Heaven and Earth
Isn't it just like a man to build something
out of nothing

then dispose of it when it no longer serves
his needs
And I'm trying to find the difference
between God and all of my
past lovers
Because lately I've been told to have faith in
their existence
although I don't see them much any more
And I have to wonder if they're simply
being led by the spirit
If we're healed by the blood, then how
careless was it for God to allow
that woman to have an issue with hers
Maybe Jesus was trying to tell us something
when he sacrificed his
What if Eve ate that apple to rid herself from
the garden but could never
quite free herself from man's control
Because there were women raped in the
Bible then later forced to marry their
attackers
Women today are still forced in convents
with their attackers
You see I think we've been getting it all
wrong
What if masculinity isn't toxic but rather
biblical…

It's like the word sometimes been way too
busy abusing the mother
So for his forgiveness
God decided to bless the child who managed
to have their own
In this Jesus wept, but no one else did
And I have to forgive myself on drunken
nights when I didn't quite say no
Forgive him for not quite hearing yes
Remind myself that woman
will always be servant
And favor is man
And I found savor,
I mean favor
In this moment just like Mary
I found favor, right?

SBIW

I no longer desire to be a
Strong Black Independent Woman
It's much too heavy of a burden to bare
I saw how it destroyed my Nana and almost
Killed all of her daughters
Maybe I'm a bit too passive
But death by suicide has never been
that appealing to me

Triggers

Last night I laid in bed underneath my lover
he looked down upon me with innocence
and purity in his eyes
Caressed my cheeks
Whispered like Sunday mourning wind
chimes on Nana's front porch he says…
You like that don't you?
His words sound like the unholy scriptures
of rapists
Triggers flashbacks when my memory's too
weak.
Chases me down dark alleys, rips off my
panties and sodomizes my clock work to
woman hood.
Transforms my "no's" into debates
bloody challenges submerged with
"I dare you"
he doesn't get that I'm toxic
Anxiety builds its way up then crawls out of
my mouth like vomit.
Tears pour down my face burning acid
he tries to wipe them off but I flinch.
Doesn't get that his touch feels like the
splintery legs of spiders
slithering their way inside of my pores then
ripping out of my flesh.

His hands look like dog muzzles wrapped
around my mouth to
silence my cries as he forces his masculinity
upon me.
But Mama says I'm overreacting
says if you don't get over your past you are
going to chase that boy away.
But he has been dancing with a corpse long
enough to recite the eulogy.
My broken frame tangles with his desires to
love me.
He waltzes with the walking dead
every time we make love
buries parts of my soul that I fight to get
back in the morning.
Rape is a butcher knife pressed into your
side telling you not to move or this will be
the last moment in life that you remember.
Hold your breath.
Don't fight back
Tell me what textures of fabric are asking
for it?
Stitches and hems versus a man's self
control and they tell me I'm overreacting.
But when Simon says **open your legs,** you
better
Innocence spilled on the steps of Catholic
Church doors

Rosary beads wrapped around my neck to
strangle my normality.
So when he asks why he can't run his
fingers through my hair
I will tell him that it's because I'm guarded.
For this I do not apologize…..
Because when the shit hits the fan no one
really bothers to ask
why the fuck were we standing that close to
the propellers in the first place?!
One in every three girls are raped
Hollow corpses walking down vacant
streets.
Did you mourn her today?
Place roses inside the body that she now
carries as a tomb.
Tell the world about all the beautiful things
she had to offer it
before man made mockery out of her
insides
You see the cops they will mention the boy
who cried wolf
but silence the girl who screams **RAPE**.
But I won't label myself a victim just to
stroke your masculinity
Instead tonight I will lay in bed underneath
my lover

Ignore the triggers crawling behind me like
shadows of the living dead and
When he asks me if I like it
I will look back into his empty eyes and
whisper….. *yes*

My Desolate Womb

In your hurry to leave
you left something behind,
something of value
Not sure if you wanted to keep it or if it
wanted to be kept
Without knowledge I must have buried it in
the deepest parts of my body for shelter
Unbeknownst to you my insides were
tainted
They couldn't hold such treasure
My interior was not designed to supply such
a sanctuary for the unborn
I am made of shards and deadly debris
sunken rubble left behind
when the bridges of London took their fall
I've learned that babies take bad falls too…
If a fetus wraps the umbilical cord around its
neck to skydive from my uterus
but no one is there to catch it
Like cracked trees in the wilderness
Does it even make a sound
Does it cry
Abandoned my abdomen
Because no one, not even someone
that is made up of half of me
wants to stick with me

Nothing good grows from graveyard gravel
I am the cemetery that no ones wants to pet
My pelvis reeks of guilt and blame
Can you smell the last man who touched
me?
The one before that who loved me and I
pushed away
Does it ooze with the memory of my
betrayer
I let the baby leave and the villains' evidence
stay
I'll cry and I'll grieve
But maybe God knew it was better this
way…

Rainbow

I covered it up
Kept silent out of my fears
Couldn't break the cycle
The Secrets
The longing weighed heavy on me like
decisions in court rooms
I deemed myself guilty
Took the verdict
without the need to plea my case
I disappeared, I shutdown
In attempts to fight my demons
I became my own damn demon
Couldn't escape the bond that bound me so
tightly to my past
But in order to change
the bond must be broken
The cycle thrown off balance
Fill out the secret to combat the depression
Fight the need to stay silent
rip off the Band-Aid to expose the wound
Uncover the root
And in this revelation, it should bring you to
loving yourself more than the bullets that
pierced your life or the stab wounds you
wear as decoration
The dark holes you crawled

into for survival
That light at the end of the trauma
is self-love.

Borrowed Bodies

Our bodies do not belong to us
hands shoved into dark holes
pulling us out of wombs that didn't belong
to our Mothers
Man saw fit to follow this nuisance
by hitting us on the backside
like our birth meant something that needed
punishment or correction
Bones broken on behalf of mankind
We find these truths to now be
government inflicted
If we obey this law
Then little girls who cross their ankles
Will grow to be women who close their legs
and not fidget
When the senate or man
Dares to pry them open
Whose mouths are shut with barbed wire
and know better than to speak
Women who are caged lions that stand next
to men who can't decipher their roar
So, we pay our tax in blood
month by month
Until the bank runs dry
Then birthed babies on Stocks
with tattered wings

Stocks that were never meant to truly fly.

24

And so it was

My mother has skin that takes the night sky
by the hand and says
"Come with me,
I'll show you that even in darkness
you can be beautiful"
And so it did
And so it was
And thank God for Black mothers who carry
just enough midnight for comfort
Thank God for Black mothers
who aren't afraid
to sit at the edge of the moon with you
Thank God for Black mothers
who would sacrifice their sun

Let's Go Home

Mama made us tend church every Sunday
to keep away from the dope boys down the
street
She'd praise God
while the choir boys looked up our dresses
I don't tend church much now
The choir boys are all in jail
and the dope boys never had no
God to turn to.

Get Right Church and Let's Go Home

Who am I?

I whispered my voice into the darkness
that blanket space between
time and a life span
Hoping the echoes of God would emerge
from shadows to come back to me
I've witness my lonely hang from the
branches of broken trees
Insanity repeats this cycle
Over and over
Reality shifts and stands still
I've slow danced with my reflection
over an open fire
then watch the dust of cinder fall
like perfect harmony
The air escapes the room and my lunges
racing towards a nothingness
that I can not find
But it calls to me
It calls to me like unheard symphonies
reminding me that I am alone
to exist in the now
To be something and nothing
I am something
I am nothing
I was an isolated moment in time

Fire Dancing

28

Sometimes I want to scream into an open fire just to see what the flames would do...........

Heroes and civilians

I've learned that when dealing with men
Regardless of race
A damsel in distress is more accepting than
a woman in full power

Maybe that's why all the damsels stay
broken.

Insomnia

Tonight I slayed the beast
Fought fire and brimstone,
looked the monster directly in the eye and
forced exit upon it.
Left no option.
Used all my strength
to cast out its presence.

When that didn't work, I lunged into the abyss
pulled out a sword
Cut it off by the head
burned the body
separated the ashes across
the four corners of the Earth.

Made it back in time by Sunset.
I climbed into bed and laid beside
my depression.
Sounds unrewarding.
But at least with anxiety gone
We can finally get some rest.

Revolving Doors

My hands are like revolving doors
Tired of waiting on someone who
will fit on the inside of the glass
No one ever actually stays on this
side of the glass, they always leave
I trained my heart to think
that this is normal.
My mind to believe it's fair
My soul to find acceptance
and my hands…….
I've tricked my hands into thinking
that this is actual sacrifice
and not torture
so you represent everything
that I would die for

The Lurking

The change was never loud
It was silent and unexpected
Always lurking in the shadows
for the chance to be seen
They would warn the masses of the
unfamiliarity it would bring
NO ONE listened
Some swore it came out of the blue
But secretly it was there all along
And once it showed its hand
there was no turning back

Yellow bricks, dirt roads

The Women in my Family
remind me of Dorothy
Never satisfied with themselves so they
leave
to find false Gods
Only to return back to where we started
Along the way they carry men
and their baggage
walk along the Solar Plexus chakra of their
deadened destiny
The women I love nurture men who don't
have the courage to love themselves
The bottom on their shoes develop scuff
marks from all the times they
chased away the lion in the dead of the
night
to ensure the peace of the morning
These women are smart
they hide behind the submission of society
longing to scare them
with the lash of a crows feather
Delicate but deadly so they do all to
preserve
These women hearts beats
like tin cans on tin roofs

Using love to unlock the strain joints of
others
But somehow they don't see
Yet seek outside validation to bring them
truth

Call it Rape

You can't call it rape
If the only witness to the attack
was the body of the accuser
When the abuser was once a lover
label this an argument turned physical
When the disagreement
grows arms, pries open your legs
Holds you down to force their will and
opinion inside of you
Even this is not rape
It's a lapse in romantic judgment
A simple heated debate
Remind yourself that he loves you
The moment was just a mistake
When the study session turns bloody
and there's no test to take insight
When the history of the account is smeared
across loose leaf
papers and rented textbooks
If you can only loosely reenact the events
Be prepared for the papers will deem you a
whore
They will place your memory on the witness
stand

can you stand to relive the assault?
Prematurely drag the skeletons from your
closet without giving them the time to dress
Now you scream naked in your truth
but no one seems to hear
Instead they will gather whispers about the
attire or lack thereof
The exposure of bones
Victims like you should always wear flesh
How else is anyone to trace the trail of
bruising that you so claim to have
I know what you must think but this simply
can't be known as rape
It was a night of anatomy
Placed on flash cards
stripped from your power
Point out the positive
You now have a better chance at passing the
pop quiz in the morning
If the victim, I mean survivor identifies as
male this is where things can get tricky so
Call it a job well done
Reward him with pats on the back
What type of normal guy doesn't want to get
laid?
So instead of filing the complaint its cause
for celebration

When she identifies as woman there is a
strong possibility she was asking for it
Ask her if she remembered the night
correctly
If alcohol was involved that cancels both
sides of the case
More specifically the side that manages to
maintain that the night was anything less
than fun
They will claim the same red bull that gave
you wings gave them permission
How could this be rape when the entire
purpose was to fly
If you choose to go to the doctor know that
rape kits aren't technically evidence
just proof that something happened
The bruises and blood could be seen as
foreplay
How can one even truly be sure unless you
call it
Unless you call it
Unless you call it by its name…..
Look the monster into the eye and say that,
yes all of this is rape
Say it out loud
How often times cat calls are the gateway
drug to sexual abuse
Say it out loud

When a no is drowned out by the wave of
hands uplifting's skirts
You can still say it if it barely hurt
They may rewrite the definition, but the act
remains the same
When a body is found raped and murdered
They will drop the rape to convict the
murder
Rape culture will turn it's bloody hand to
convince you of it's justice
And take away the very reason the person
was turned into a corpse in the first place
When your shamed into giving your body
over
It is rape
When you thought you wanted it, you
changed your mind, but the person kept
going
Yes, call it rape
When you give in to the monsters that lurk
behind your bushes
because it's easier to do that than say no
Yes, that is indeed rape
When you've drank away your
consciousness
You weren't sober enough to consent
They will try to convince you

that your body was nothing more than a
party favor
Don't give in to their notion
Call this rape
If your safety lies within you taking off your
pants
When the threat of violence lays quietly
beside your pillow case
There is no such things as gentle rape
Rape is rape
This is rape
Call it rape
I was once raped

My mother bound together capes
with old dishrags and
mismatched socks
placed them around me and my
sibling's neck to say,
Quit crying
This world ain't gone save you
You better damn sure learn how to
save yourself

Hidden Landscapes

What if they find us? He says

They won't…..
for in this realm I have created a landscape
invisible to the eye
It is a place where children like me and you
can exist with full bellies
and empty sorrows
Food is overflowing
The beds are always warm and they
somehow make themselves
A place where they can't touch us
with racism or boarders
Where weapons are never bought
because no one ever actually makes them
The ability to read
and the people are free
Free to choose
Free to love
Where hugs are only given with permission
No one questions identity or the need to be
anything other than who we truly are

*If a place like that exists, why must we keep
it hidden?* He asks.

Because we don't allow adults here
Some children grow up to be bad people
and if they find this place then truly

they will taint the landscape

Na'Tosha De'Von was born in Chicago, Illinois with a rich upbringing in Kosciusko, Mississippi. The actor and poet holds an MFA in Acting from the University of Arkansas as well as a Bachelor's degree in Speech Communication and Theatre from Jackson State University. Na'Tosha got her start in poetry as a young girl using it as a method of healing and self-discovery. Na'Tosha currently resides in Northwest Arkansas and spends her spare time going to museums and listening to jazz music.

Thank you to the Mid-America Arts Alliance and the Artist 360 grant. Without your generosity and support this book would not be possible.

Thank you to Archie Kern Jr. for your endless support and sponsorship.